anythink

D0579395

MAPS

Pebble® Plus

Map Scales

by
Jennifer M. Besel

Consulting editor:
Gail Saunders-Smith, PhD

Consultant:
Dr. Sarah E. Battersby
Department of Geography
University of South Carolina

CAPSTONE PRESS
a capstone imprint

Pebble Plus is published by Capstone Press,
1710 Roe Crest Drive, North Mankato, Minnesota 56003
www.capstonepub.com

Library of Congress Cataloging-in-Publication Data
Besel, Jennifer M.
Map scales / by Jennifer M. Besel.
pages cm.—(Pebble plus. Maps)
Includes bibliographical references and index.
Summary: "Simple text with full-color photos and illustrations provide basic information about
map scales"—Provided by publisher.
ISBN 978-1-4765-3083-3 (library binding)—ISBN 978-1-4765-3505-0 (ebook pdf)—ISBN 978-1-4765-3523-4 (paperback)
1. Map scales—Juvenile literature. I. Title.
GA118.B47 2014
912.01'48—dc23   2012049387

Editorial Credits
Gene Bentdahl, designer; Kathy McColley, production specialist; Sarah Schuette, photo stylist; Marcy Morin, scheduler

Photo Credits
Capstone: 7, 11, 15, 19; Capstone Studio: Karon Dubke, cover, 1, 5, 9, 13, 17, 21

Note to Parents and Teachers

The Maps set supports social studies standards related to people, places, and environments. This
book describes and illustrates map scales. The images support early readers in understanding the
text. The repetition of words and phrases helps early readers learn new words. This book also
introduces early readers to subject-specific vocabulary words, which are defined in the Glossary
section. Early readers may need assistance to read some words and to use the Table of Contents,
Glossary, Read More, Internet Sites, and Index sections of the book.

Printed in the United States of America in North Mankato, Minnesota.
032013   007223CGF13

Table of Contents

It's Too Short!

Distances on maps and globes

look much shorter

than they are on Earth.

How can you tell

how far away a place is?

Every map has a scale.

A map's scale compares

distances on the map

to distances on Earth.

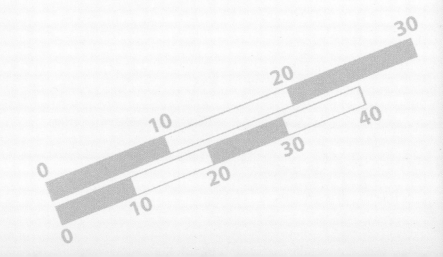

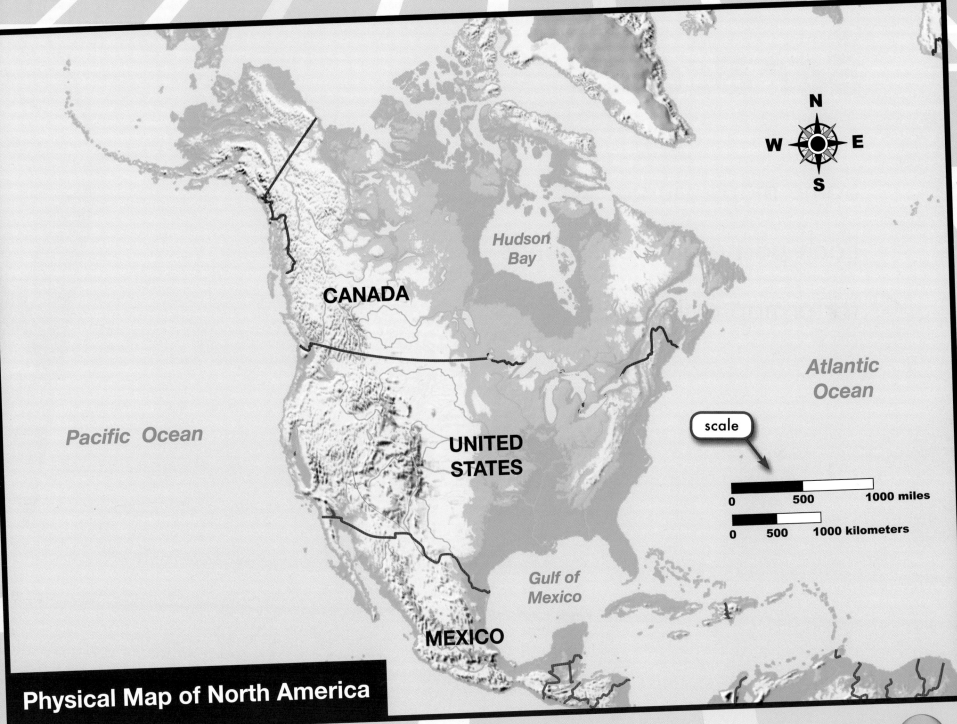

N
W E
S

Hudson
Bay

CANADA

Pacific Ocean

UNITED
STATES

Atlantic
Ocean

scale

| 0 | 500 | 1000 miles |

| 0 | 500 | 1000 kilometers |

Gulf of
Mexico

MEXICO

Physical Map of North America

Bar Scales

Some maps use bar scales.

Each part on the bar stands

for a map distance.

Washington
Elementary
School

Key

school

house

playground

tree

N
W   E
S

50 feet

18 meters

Look at the numbers
under a bar scale.
They tell what distance
the parts equal on Earth.

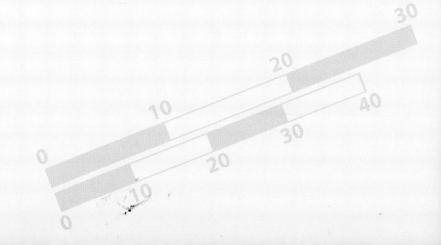

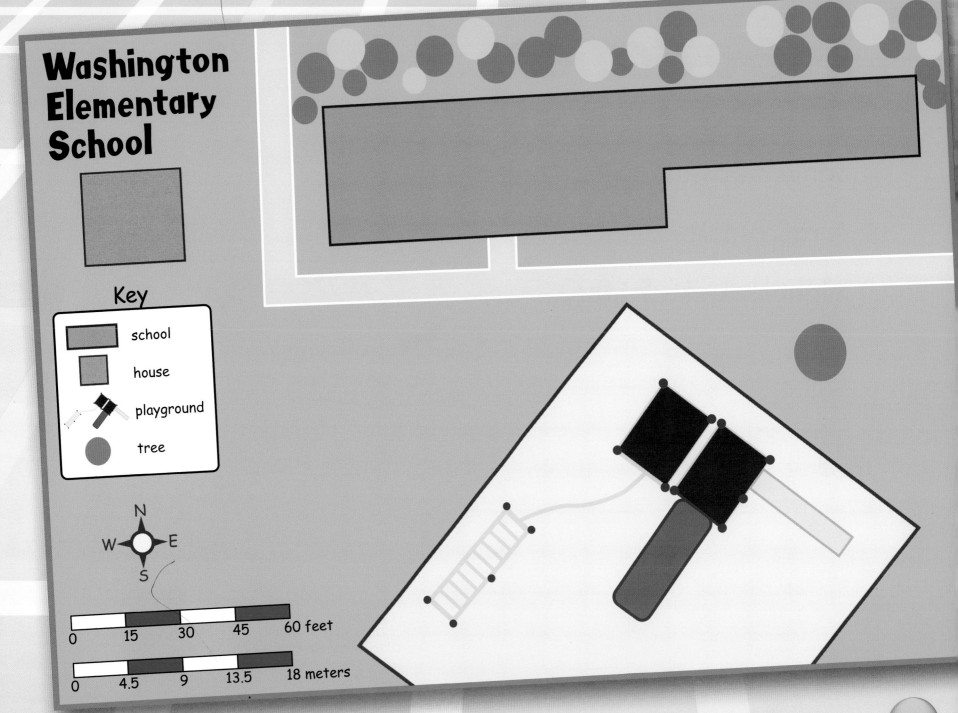

Washington Elementary School

Key

- school
- house
- playground
- tree

N W E S

| 0 | 15 | 30 | 45 | 60 feet |

| 0 | 4.5 | 9 | 13.5 | 18 meters |

Ratio Scales

Some maps use ratio scales.

A ratio scale

might look like 1:1,000.

To read the ratio scale say,

"one to one thousand."

It means 1 unit of measure

on the map equals

1,000 units on Earth.

Velociraptor

Spinosaurus

Triceratops

Tyrannosaurus Rex

Stegosaurus

Phororhacos

Tylosaurus

Scale
1:1,000

Brachiosaurus

Pterodactyl

Walk with the
Dinosaurs

Word Scales

Some maps use words

to compare map distances

to real distances.

YELLOWSTONE NATIONAL PARK

▲ Campsite
■ Place of interest
● Town

1 inch equals 10 miles

N
W · E
S

Cooke City
Silver Gate

Gardiner

Mammoth Hot Springs
Tower Ranger Station and Roosevelt National Historic District

Canyon Village

Norris Geyser Basin

Madison Junction

Fishing Bridge
Lake Village

West Yellowstone

Yellowstone Lake

Old Faithful
West Thumb
West Thumb

Shoshone Lake

Lewis Lake
Heart Lake

17

A word scale might say,

"1 inch equals 10 miles."

That means every inch

on the map equals

10 miles on Earth.

YELLOWSTONE NATIONAL PARK

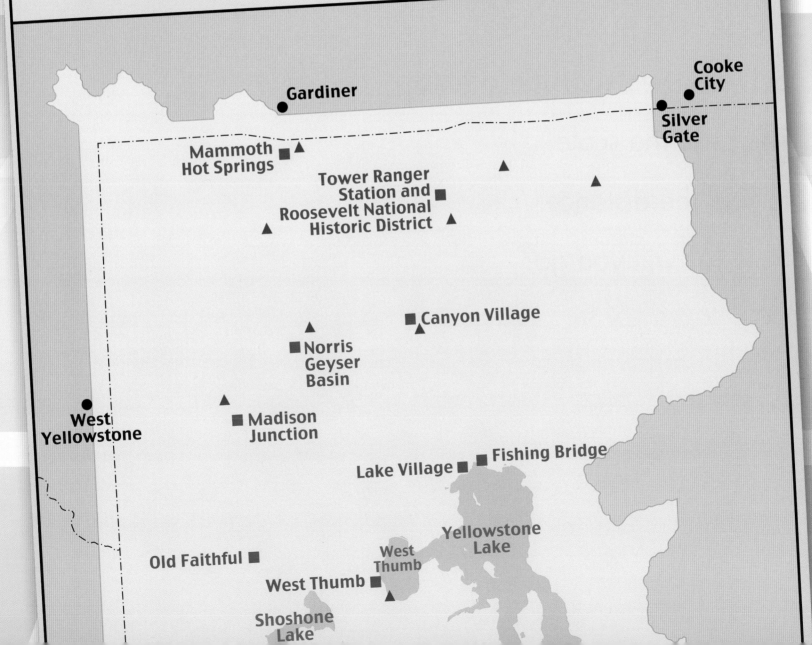

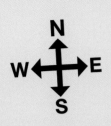

▲ Campsite

■ Place of interest

● Town

1 inch equals 10 miles

N
W ← → E
S

Cooke City

Gardiner

Silver Gate

Mammoth Hot Springs

Tower Ranger Station and Roosevelt National Historic District

Canyon Village

Norris Geyser Basin

West Yellowstone

Madison Junction

Fishing Bridge

Lake Village

Yellowstone Lake

Old Faithful

West Thumb

West Thumb

Shoshone Lake

Use a ruler to measure

between two spots on a map.

Then use the scale

to find the distance.

How far will you go?

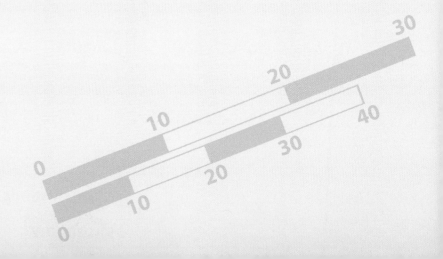

Glossary

compare—to judge one thing against another

distance—the amount of space between two places

equal—the same as something else in size or amount

globe—a round model of the world

ratio—two numbers that are compared to each other

unit of measure—an amount that is used to find the size of something; an inch is a unit of measure

Read More

Besel, Jennifer M. *Symbols and Keys.* Maps. North Mankato, Minn.: Capstone Press, 2014.

Spilsbury, Louise. *Mapping.* Investigate. Chicago: Heinemann Library, 2010.

Wade, Mary Dodson. *Map Scales.* Rookie Read-about Geography. New York: Children's Press, 2013.

Internet Sites

FactHound offers a safe, fun way to find Internet sites related to this book. All of the sites on FactHound have been researched by our staff.

Here's all you do:

Visit *www.facthound.com*

Type in this code: 9781476530833

Super-cool stuff! Check out projects, games and lots more at **www.capstonekids.com**

23

Critical Thinking Using the Common Core

1. Look at the map on page 19. How many miles is it from Mammoth Hot Springs to Old Faithful? Describe how you found your answer. (Craft and Structure)

2. How do the sizes of places on maps compare to their actual sizes? Using the map and scale on page 7, figure out how many miles the United States is from east to west. Compare that distance to the size of Mexico. (Craft and Structure, Key Ideas and Details)

Index

Word Count: 165
Grade: 1
Early-Intervention Level: 17